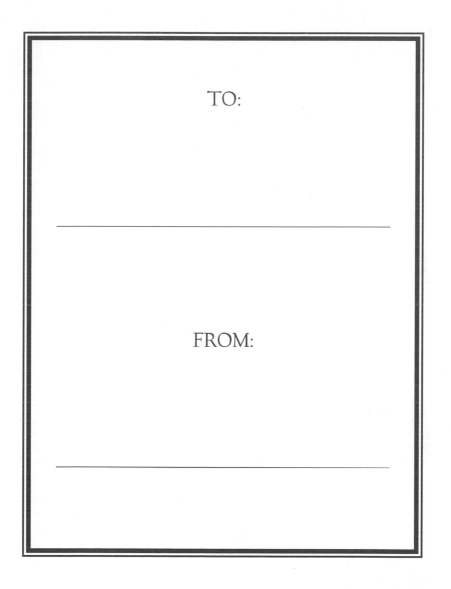

TO:

_____

FROM:

_____

C. S. Lewis

THE
C. S. LEWIS
JOURNAL

Edited by Patricia S. Klein

HarperSanFrancisco
A Division of HarperCollins*Publishers*

HarperCollins books may be purchased for educational, business, or sales promotional use. For information please write: Special Markets Department, HarperCollins Publishers, 10 East 53rd Street, New York, NY 10022.

HarperCollins Web site: http://www.harpercollins.com
HarperCollins®, ▟®, and HarperSanFrancisco™ are
trademarks of HarperCollins Publishers

FIRST EDITION
Designed by Joseph Rutt

Printed in China

Library of Congress Cataloging-in-Publication Data is available.

ISBN-13: 978-0-06-089188-6
ISBN-10: 0-06-089188-2

06 07 08 09 10 SCP 10 9 8 7 6 5 4 3 2 1

Introduction

⤞⤝⤞

Most people are reluctant to lend books from their libraries because they're afraid said books will not be returned. Over the years, as a self-confessed bibliomaniac, I have discovered that I am happy to loan out my books, but I always do so with specific instructions: "Please don't mark the book in ink." For me, the impulse to mark in a book—to note special passages, identify critical arguments, celebrate a great turn of phrase—is irresistible. I understand that. What brings me to my knees, breaks my heart (and possibly friendships), is not the marking, but the ink. I've even offered pencils with my lent books to reenforce my point.

The best books are read with a pencil at hand. Because reading is such an intimate thing, mind touching mind, or soul touching soul, very often we need to mark the passages that touch us, the places we want to revisit. Have you ever picked up a book from your shelf, read many years before, and much to your delight, found notes and markings from past readings? Like old photographs and letters, these notes remind us of the ideas and characters we've met and enjoyed and loved before in our lives.

I'll wager that most of us have marked up at least one book by C. S. Lewis. While he is most recognized as the author of the beloved children's fantasy series The Chronicles of Narnia, he also has a great body of writing in a variety of fields: adult fiction, poetry, English literature, and popular theology. Unlike many books that line library shelves, his are books that we are happy to revisit regularly. His are books that offer new discoveries and fresh perspectives, even in the third and fourth readings. His are books where we know we will encounter a vibrant and energetic spirituality, where we are not coddled and pandered to, but where we are always challenged and dared to meet the Creator of the Universe and to consider the Eternal over the temporal.

Among Lewis's most compelling writings are his letters. He was a disciplined and faithful correspondent, whose letters are filled with humor and compassion, encouragement and instruction. We glimpse a man who we'd really like to know, someone we wish we could write to, someone who could answer a question or explain a difficult idea. But we must settle for marking the book, asking our questions in the margins, encoding our queries and surprises with penciled question marks and exclamation points.

One of the intentions of this journal is to offer an opportunity to satisfy our impulse to engage Lewis—to respond, to explore, to argue, to examine. Rather than settling for writing in the margins, we have here space to consider not simply his writings but also our response to those writings. Herein are pieces from a great variety of his works, written across the span of his lifetime. Included are some of his most memorable and recognizable writings, as well as some of the more obscure and less often read. But all compel a response.

As a very young man, Lewis wrote to childhood friend Arthur Greeves: "Whenever you are fed up with life, start writing: ink is the great cure for all human ills, as I have found out long ago." Lewis understood the transforming power of writing, the power of developing an idea on paper or wrestling a difficult emotion or creating a memorable character. His counsel to his friend is appropriate to this book as well: ". . . ink is the great cure for all human ills." In this journal may we find some healing, encounter some surprises, and battle some dragons. And please, feel free to write in ink.

Patricia S. Klein, editor

6th line clinic ~ Dr Stern ~ Rec ~ clinic 4 ~ 730 M-F
905.847 8050

Hiding in Plain Sight

We may ignore, but we can nowhere evade, the presence of God. The world is crowded with Him. He walks everywhere *incognito*. And the *incognito* is not always hard to penetrate. The real labour is to remember, to attend. In fact, to come awake. Still more, to remain awake.

—from *Letters to Malcolm: Chiefly on Prayer*

[illegible] is He knows anyway
talk to Him about it. There are
two in this relationship. The
intimacy we crave is only
accomplished through effort
not struggle but consistent effort.
When I misplaced my earring and
Katie's crucifix I turned the
living upside down — this is how
I should feel when I'm searching
for the Lord. There is nothing more
important, nothing means more.
Yet the rocks cry out — we
know at every level that He
reigns that He knows all things
The mailbox belonging to Dr O Sullivan's
office is full — please hang up
4-730
9-5 M-F

Melchizedek (King of Righteousness)
a type or figure of the royalty and eternal
priesthood of Jesus Christ
We stand on your authority and at
the sound of your name darkness flees.
You sit at the Father's right hand.

What Do I Do Next?

I come back to St. John: 'if our heart condemn us, God is greater than our heart'. And equally, 'if our heart flatter us, God is greater than our heart'. I sometimes pray not for self-knowledge in general but for just so much self-knowledge at the moment as I can bear and use at the moment; the little daily dose.

Have we any reason to suppose that total self-knowledge, if it were given us, would be for our good? Children and fools, we are told, should never look at half-done work; and we are not yet, I trust, even half-done. You and I wouldn't, at all stages, think it wise to tell a pupil exactly what we thought of his quality. It is much more important that he should know what to do next.

—from *Letters to Malcolm: Chiefly on Prayer*

Being in the Presence of God

Whenever we find that our religious life is making us feel that we are good—above all, that we are better than someone else—I think we may be sure that we are being acted on, not by God, but by the devil. The real test of being in the presence of God is, that you either forget about yourself altogether or see yourself as a small, dirty object. It is better to forget about yourself altogether.

—from *Mere Christianity*

What Is Real Life?

The great thing, if one can, is to stop regarding all the unpleasant things as interruptions of one's 'own', or 'real' life. The truth is of course that what one calls the interruptions are precisely one's real life—the life God is sending one day by day: what one calls one's 'real life' is a phantom of one's own imagination.

—from a letter to Arthur Greeves, 20 December 1943

For Me Alone

Be sure that the ins and outs of your individuality are no mystery to Him; and one day they will no longer be a mystery to you. The mould in which a key is made would be a strange thing, if you had never seen a key: and the key itself a strange thing if you had never seen a lock. Your soul has a curious shape because it is a hollow made to fit a particular swelling in the infinite contours of the Divine substance, or a key to unlock one of the doors in the house with many mansions. For it is not humanity in the abstract that is to be saved, but you—you, the individual reader, John Stubbs or Janet Smith. Blessed and fortunate creature, your eyes shall behold Him and not another's. . . . Your place in heaven will seem to be made for you and you alone, because you were made for it—made for it stitch by stitch as a glove is made for a hand.

—from *The Problem of Pain*

So, What Have I Chosen?

L aw, in his terrible, cool voice, said, . . . 'If you have not chosen the Kingdom of God, it will make in the end no difference what you have chosen instead'. Those are hard words to take. Will it really make no difference whether it was women or patriotism, cocaine or art, whisky or a seat in the Cabinet, money or science? Well, surely no difference that matters. We shall have missed the end for which we are formed and rejected the only thing that satisfies. Does it matter to a man dying in a desert by which choice of route he missed the only well?

—from 'A Slip of the Tongue' in *The Weight of Glory*

Am I Ready to Give Him Everything?

It is not so much of our time and so much of our attention that God demands; it is not even all our time and all our attention; it is ourselves. For each of us the Baptist's words are true: 'He must increase and I decrease'. He will be infinitely merciful to our repeated failures; I know no promise that He will accept a deliberate compromise. For He has, in the last resort, nothing to give us but Himself; and He can give that only insofar as our self-affirming will retires and makes room for Him in our souls. Let us make up our minds to it; there will be nothing 'of our own' left over to live on, no 'ordinary' life. . . . For He claims all, because He is love and must bless. He cannot bless us unless He has us. When we try to keep within us an area that is our own, we try to keep an area of death. Therefore, in love, He claims all. There's no bargaining with Him.

—from 'A Slip of the Tongue' in *The Weight of Glory*

At What Cost?

We are not necessarily doubting that God will do the best for us;
we are wondering how painful the best will turn out to be.

—from a letter to Father Peter Bide, 29 April 1959

_____

_____

_____

_____

_____

_____

_____

_____

_____

_____

_____

_____

_____

_____

_____

_____

Why Is Prayer a Duty?

Well, let's now at any rate come clean. Prayer is irksome. An excuse to omit it is never unwelcome. When it is over, this casts a feeling of relief and holiday over the rest of the day. We are reluctant to begin. We are delighted to finish. While we are at prayer, but not while we are reading a novel or solving a cross-word puzzle, any trifle is enough to distract us. . . .

Now the disquieting thing is not simply that we skimp and begrudge the duty of prayer. The really disquieting thing is it should have to be numbered among duties at all. For we believe that we were created 'to glorify God and enjoy Him forever'. And if the few, the very few, minutes we now spend on intercourse with God are a burden to us rather than a delight, what then? . . .

The painful effort which prayer involves is no proof that we are doing something we were not created to do.

If we were perfected, prayer would not be a duty, it would be delight. Some day, please God, it will be.

—from *Letters to Malcolm: Chiefly on Prayer*

Does God Answer Prayer?

Prayers are not always—in the crude, factual sense of the word—'granted'. This is not because prayer is a weaker kind of causality, but because it is a stronger kind. When it 'works' at all it works unlimited by space and time. That is why God has retained a discretionary power of granting or refusing it; except on that condition prayer would destroy us. It is not unreasonable for a headmaster to say, 'Such and such things you may do according to the fixed rules of this school. But such and such other things are too dangerous to be left to general rules. If you want to do them you must come and make a request and talk over the whole matter with me in my study. And then—we'll see'.

—from 'Work and Prayer' in *God in the Dock*

Am I Listening?

Do our prayers sometimes go wrong because we insist on trying to talk to God when He wants to talk to us. Joy tells me that once, years ago, she was haunted one morning by a feeling that God wanted something of her, a persistent pressure like the nag of a neglected duty. And until mid-morning she kept on wondering what it was. But the moment she stopped worrying, the answer came through as plain as a spoken voice. It was 'I don't want you to *do* anything. I want to *give* you something'; and immediately her heart was full of peace and delight. St. Augustine says 'God gives where He finds empty hands'. A man whose hands are full of parcels can't receive a gift. Perhaps these parcels are not always sins or earthly cares, but sometimes our own fussy attempts to worship Him in *our* way.

—from a letter to an American lady, 31 March 1958

Misgivings

Just as the Christian has his moments when the clamour of this visible and audible world is so persistent and the whisper of the spiritual world so faint that faith and reason can hardly stick to their guns, so, as I well remember, the atheist too has his moments of shuddering misgiving, of an all but irresistible suspicion that old tales may after all be true, that something or someone from outside may at any moment break into his neat, explicable, mechanical universe. Believe in God and you will have to face hours when it seems *obvious* that this material world is the only reality: disbelieve in Him and you must face hours when this material world seems to shout at you that it is *not* all. No conviction, religious or irreligious, will, of itself, end once and for all this fifth-columnist in the soul. Only the practice of Faith resulting in the habit of Faith will gradually do that.

—from 'Religion: Reality or Substitute?' in *Christian Reflections*

For Emergency Use Only

Everyone has noticed how hard it is to turn our thoughts to God when everything is going well with us. We 'have all we want' is a terrible saying when 'all' does not include God. We find God an interruption. As St. Augustine says somewhere, 'God wants to give us something, but cannot, because our hands are full—there's nowhere for Him to put it.' Or as a friend of mine said, 'We regard God as an airman regards his parachute; it's there for emergencies but he hopes he'll never have to use it.' Now God, who has made us, knows what we are and that our happiness lies in Him. Yet we will not seek it in Him as long as He leaves us any other resort where it can even plausibly be looked for. While what we call 'our own life' remains agreeable we will not surrender it to Him. What then can God do in our interests but make 'our own life' less agreeable to us, and take away the plausible source of false happiness?

—from *The Problem of Pain*

May I Be Rich, Please?

Christ said it was difficult for 'the rich' to enter the Kingdom of Heaven, referring, no doubt, to 'riches' in the ordinary sense. But I think it really covers riches in every sense—good fortune, health, popularity, and all the things one wants to have. All these things tend—just as money tends—to make you feel independent of God, because if you have them you are happy already and contented in this life. You don't want to turn away to anything more, and so you try to rest in a shadowy happiness as if it could last for ever. But God wants to give you a real and eternal happiness. Consequently He may have to take all these 'riches' away from you: if He doesn't, you will go on relying on them.

—from 'Answers to Questions on Christianity' in *God in the Dock*

Every Day, Begin Again

As you say, the thing is to rely *only* on God. The time will come when you will regard all this misery as a small price to pay for having been brought to that dependence. Meanwhile (don't I know) the trouble is that relying on God has to begin all over again every day as if nothing had yet been done. . . .

—from a letter to 'Mrs. Lockley', 12 (?) September 1949

What Do I Choose?

God gives what He has, not what He has not: He gives the happiness that there is, not the happiness that is not. To be God—to be like God and to share His goodness in creaturely response—to be miserable—these are the only three alternatives. If we will not learn to eat the only food that the universe grows—the only food that any possible universe ever can grow—then we must starve eternally.

—from *The Problem of Pain*

_____

_____

_____

_____

_____

_____

_____

_____

_____

_____

_____

_____

Do I Forgive Myself?

I think that if God forgives us we must forgive ourselves. Otherwise it is almost like setting up ourselves as a higher tribunal than Him.

—from a letter to Miss Breckenridge, 19 April 1951

Seventy Times Seven

There is no use in talking as if forgiveness were easy. We all know the old joke, 'You've given up smoking once; I've given it up a dozen times'. In the same way I could say of a certain man, 'Have I forgiven him for what he did that day? I've forgiven him more times than I can count'. For we find that the work of forgiveness has to be done over and over again. We forgive, we mortify our resentment; a week later some chain of thought carries us back to the original offence and we discover the old resentment blazing away as if nothing had been done about it at all. We need to forgive our brother seventy times seven not only for 490 offences but for one offence.

—from *Reflections on the Psalms*

Divine Abdication

For He seems to do nothing of Himself which He can possibly delegate to His creatures. He commands us to do slowly and blunderingly what He could do perfectly and in the twinkling of an eye. He allows us to neglect what He would have us do, or to fail. Perhaps we do not fully realise the problem, so to call it, of enabling finite free wills to co-exist with Omnipotence. It seems to involve at every moment almost a sort of divine abdication. We are not mere recipients or spectators. We are either privileged to share the game or compelled to collaborate in the work, 'to wield our little tridents'. Is this amazing process simply Creation going on before our eyes? This is how (no light matter) God makes something—indeed, makes gods—out of nothing.

—from 'The Efficacy of Prayer' in *The World's Last Night*

A Gradual Decline

Christianity asserts that every individual human being is going to live for ever, and this must be either true or false. Now there are a good many things which would not be worth bothering about if I were going to live only seventy years, but which I had better bother about very seriously if I am going to live for ever. Perhaps my bad temper or my jealousy are gradually getting worse—so gradually that the increase in seventy years will not be very noticeable. But it might be absolute hell in a million years: in fact, if Christianity is true, Hell is the precisely correct technical term for what it would be.

—from *Mere Christianity*

Strategic Errors

Good and evil both increase at compound interest. That is why the little decisions you and I make every day are of such infinite importance. The smallest good act today is the capture of a strategic point from which, a few months later, you may be able to go on to victories you never dreamed of. An apparently trivial indulgence in lust or anger today is the loss of a ridge or railway line or bridgehead from which the enemy may launch an attack otherwise impossible.

—from *Mere Christianity*

Why Did I Think This Would Be Easy?

No man knows how bad he is till he has tried very hard to be good. A silly idea is current that good people do not know what temptation means. This is an obvious lie. Only those who try to resist temptation know how strong it is. After all, you find out the strength of the German army by fighting against it, not by giving in. You find out the strength of a wind by trying to talk against it, not by lying down. A man who gives in to temptation after five minutes simply does not know what it would have been like an hour later. . . . We never find out the strength of the evil impulse inside us until we try to fight it.

—from *Mere Christianity*

Have I Given Up?

I know all about the despair of overcoming chronic temptations. It is not serious, provided self-offended petulance, annoyance at breaking records, impatience etc. don't get the upper hand. *No amount* of falls will really undo us if we keep on picking ourselves up each time. We shall of course be v. muddy and tattered children by the time we reach home. But the bathrooms are all ready, the towels put out, and the clean clothes in the airing cupboard. The only fatal thing is to lose one's temper and give it up. It is when we notice the dirt that God is most present in us; it is the v. sign of His presence. . . .

—from a letter to Mary Neylen, 20 January 1942

What Do I Enjoy?

Screwtape refines his advice to Wormwood: I would make it a rule to eradicate from my patient any strong personal taste which is not actually a sin, even if it is something quite trivial such as a fondness for county cricket or collecting stamps or drinking cocoa. Such things, I grant you, have nothing of virtue in them; but there is a sort of innocence and humility and self-forgetfulness about them which I distrust. The man who truly and disinterestedly enjoys any one thing in the world, for its own sake, and without caring two-pence what other people say about it, is by that very fact forearmed against some of our subtlest modes of attack. You should always try to make the patient abandon the people or food or books he really likes in favour of the 'best' people, the 'right' food, the 'important' books. I have known a human defended from strong temptations to social ambition by a still stronger taste for tripe and onions.

—from *The Screwtape Letters*

The Subtle Lure

Lead us not into temptation' often means, among other things, 'Deny me those gratifying invitations, those highly interesting contacts, that participation in the brilliant movements of our age, which I so often, at such risk, desire'.

—from *Reflections on the Psalms*

Diminishing Returns

Screwtape twists the gift of pleasure: Never forget that when we are dealing with any pleasure in its healthy and normal and satisfying form, we are, in a sense, on the Enemy's ground. I know we have won many a soul through pleasure. All the same, it is His invention, not ours. He made the pleasures: all our research so far has not enabled us to produce one. All we can do is to encourage the humans to take the pleasures which our Enemy has produced, at times, or in ways, or in degrees, which He has forbidden. Hence we always try to work away from the natural condition of any pleasure to that in which it is least natural, least redolent of its Maker, and least pleasurable. An ever increasing craving for an ever diminishing pleasure is the formula. It is more certain; and it's better *style*. To get the man's soul and give him *nothing* in return—that is what really gladdens Our Father's heart.

—from *The Screwtape Letters*

Have I Tasted and Seen?

William Law remarks that people are merely 'amusing themselves' by asking for the patience which a famine or a persecution would call for if, in the meantime, the weather and every other inconvenience sets them grumbling. One must learn to walk before one can run. So here. We—or at least I—shall not be able to adore God on the highest occasions if we have learned no habit of doing so on the lowest. At best, our faith and reason will tell us that He is adorable, but we shall not have *found* Him so, not have 'tasted and seen'. Any patch of sunlight in a wood will show you something about the sun which you could never get from reading books on astronomy. These pure and spontaneous pleasures are 'patches of Godlight' in the woods of our experience.

—from *Letters to Malcolm: Chiefly on Prayer*

_____

_____

_____

_____

_____

_____

_____

_____

What Are God's Intentions?

A man can no more diminish God's glory by refusing to worship Him than a lunatic can put out the sun by scribbling the word 'darkness' on the walls of his cell. But God wills our good, and our good is to love Him (with that responsive love proper to creatures) and to love Him we must know Him: and if we know Him, we shall in fact fall on our faces. If we do not, that only shows that what we are trying to love is not yet God—though it may be the nearest approximation to God which our thought and fantasy can attain. Yet the call is not only to prostration and awe; it is to a reflection of the Divine life, a creaturely participation in the Divine attributes which is far beyond our present desires. We are bidden to 'put on Christ', to become like God. That is, whether we like it or not, God intends to give us what we need, not what we now think we want. Once more, we are embarrassed by the intolerable compliment, by too much love, not too little.

—from *The Problem of Pain*

Do I Love God?

Some writers use the word charity to describe not only Christian love between human beings, but also God's love for man and man's love for God. About the second of these two, people are often worried. They are told they ought to love God. They cannot find any such feeling in themselves. What are they to do? The answer is the same as before. Act as if you did. Do not sit trying to manufacture feelings. Ask yourself, 'If I were sure that I loved God, what would I do?' When you have found the answer, go and do it.

—from *Mere Christianity*

Is It Just My Imagination?

We read of spiritual efforts, and our imagination makes us believe that, because we enjoy the idea of doing them, we have done them. I am appalled to see how much of the change wh. I thought I had undergone lately was only imaginary. The real work seems still to be done. It is so fatally easy to confuse an aesthetic appreciation of the spiritual life with the life itself—to dream that you have waked, washed, and dressed, & then to find yourself still in bed.

—from a letter to Arthur Greeves, 15 June 1930

What Do I Like to Do?

Remember that there are only three kinds of things anyone need ever do. (1) Things we *ought* to do. (2) Things we've *got* to do. (3) Things we *like* doing. I say this because some people seem to spend so much of their time doing things for none of these reasons, things like reading books they don't like because other people read them. Things you ought to do are things like doing one's work in school, or being nice to other people. Things one has got to do are things like dressing and undressing, or household shopping. Things one likes doing—but of course I don't know what *you* like. Perhaps you'll write and tell me one day.

—from a letter to Sarah (a goddaughter), 3 April 1949

Am I Proud?

If you want to find out how proud you are the easiest way is to ask yourself, 'How much do I dislike it when other people snub me, or refuse to take any notice of me, or shove their oar in, or patronise me, or show off?' The point is that each person's pride is in competition with every one else's pride. It is because I wanted to be the big noise at the party that I am so annoyed at someone else being the big noise. . . . Now what you want to get clear is that Pride is *essentially competitive*—is competitive by its very nature—while the other vices are competitive only, so to speak, by accident. Pride gets no pleasure out of having something, only out of having more of it than the next man. We say that people are proud of being rich, or clever, or good-looking, but they are not. They are proud of being richer, or cleverer, or better-looking than others. If everyone else became equally rich, or clever, or good-looking there would be nothing to be proud about. It is the comparison that makes you proud: the pleasure of being above the rest.

—from *Mere Christianity*

Delusional Thinking

Screwtape observes: No man who says *I'm as good as you* believes it. He would not say it if he did. The St. Bernard never says it to the toy dog, nor the scholar to the dunce, nor the employable to the bum, nor the pretty woman to the plain. The claim to equality, outside the strictly political field, is made only by those who feel themselves to be in some way inferior. What it expresses is precisely the itching, smarting, writhing awareness of an inferiority which the patient refuses to accept.

And therefore resents. Yes, and therefore resents every kind of superiority in others; denigrates it; wishes its annihilation. Presently he suspects every mere difference of being a claim to superiority.

—from 'Screwtape Proposes a Toast' in *The Screwtape Letters*

_____

_____

_____

_____

_____

_____

_____

_____

_____

What Is My Choice?

The Teacher points out: 'There are only two kinds of people in the end: those who say to God, "Thy will be done", and those to whom God says, in the end, "*Thy* will be done". All that are in Hell, choose it. Without that self-choice there could be no Hell. No soul that seriously and constantly desires joy will ever miss it. Those who seek find. To those who knock it is opened'.

—from *The Great Divorce*

Am I Simply a Servant or Am I an Heir?

Screwtape lays it out for Wormwood: To us a human is primarily food; our aim is the absorption of its will into ours, the increase of our own area of selfhood at its expense. But the obedience which the Enemy demands of men is quite a different thing. One must face the fact that all the talk about His love for men, and His service being perfect freedom, is not (as one would gladly believe) mere propaganda, but an appalling truth. He really *does* want to fill the universe with a lot of loathsome little replicas of Himself—creatures whose life, on its miniature scale, will be qualitatively like His own, not because He has absorbed them but because their wills freely conform to His. We want cattle who can finally become food; He wants servants who can finally become sons. We want to suck in, He wants to give out. We are empty and would be filled; He is full and flows over. Our war aim is a world in which Our Father Below has drawn all other beings into himself: the Enemy wants a world full of beings united to Him but still distinct.

—from *The Screwtape Letters*

Close-Fisted, Teeth Clenched

The Teacher explains: 'For a damned soul is nearly nothing: it is shrunk, shut up in itself. Good beats upon the damned incessantly as sound waves beat on the ears of the deaf, but they cannot receive it. Their fists are clenched, their teeth are clenched, their eyes fast shut. First they will not, in the end they cannot, open their hands for gifts, or their mouth for food, or their eyes to see'.

—from *The Great Divorce*

Can My Heart Be Broken?

To love at all is to be vulnerable. Love anything, and your heart will certainly be wrung and possibly broken. If you want to make sure of keeping it intact, you must give your heart to no one, not even to an animal. Wrap it carefully round with hobbies and little luxuries; avoid all entanglements; lock it up safe in the casket or coffin of your selfishness. But in that casket—safe, dark, motionless, airless—it will change. It will not be broken; it will become unbreakable, impenetrable, irredeemable. The alternative to tragedy, or at least to the risk of tragedy, is damnation. The only place outside Heaven where you can be perfectly safe from all the dangers and perturbations of love is Hell.

—from *The Four Loves*

Come In Out of the Wind

The real problem of the Christian life comes where people do not usually look for it. It comes the very moment you wake up each morning. All your wishes and hopes for the day rush at you like wild animals. And the first job each morning consists simply in shoving them all back; in listening to that other voice, taking that other point of view, letting that other larger, stronger, quieter life come flowing in. And so on, all day. Standing back from all your natural fussings and frettings; coming in out of the wind.

We can only do it for moments at first. But from those moments the new sort of life will be spreading through our system: because now we are letting Him work at the right part of us. It is the difference between paint, which is merely laid on the surface, and a dye or stain which soaks right through. He never talked vague, idealistic gas. When He said, 'Be perfect', He meant it. He meant that we must go in for the full treatment.

—from *Mere Christianity*

Am I Avoiding God?

If God . . . exists, mere movement in space will never bring you any nearer to Him or any farther from Him than you are at this very moment. . . .

How, then, it may be asked, can we either reach or avoid Him?

The avoiding, in many times and places, has proved so difficult that a very large part of the human race failed to achieve it. But in our own time and place it is extremely easy. Avoid silence, avoid solitude, avoid any train of thought that leads off the beaten track. Concentrate on money, sex, status, health and (above all) on your own grievances. Keep the radio on. Live in a crowd. Use plenty of sedation. If you must read books, select them very carefully. But you'd be safer to stick to the papers. You'll find the advertisements helpful; especially those with a sexy or a snobbish appeal.

About the reaching, I am a far less reliable guide. That is because I never had the experience of looking for God. It was the other way round; He was the hunter (or so it seemed to me) and I was the deer. He stalked me . . . took unerring aim, and fired.

—from 'The Seeing Eye' in *Christian Reflections*

_____

_____

_____

_____

_____

_____

_____

Is Mine a 'Willing Submission'?

Fallen man is not simply an imperfect creature who needs improvement: he is a rebel who must lay down his arms. Laying down your arms, surrendering, saying you are sorry, realising that you have been on the wrong track and getting ready to start life over again from the ground floor—that is the only way out of our 'hole'. This process of surrender—this movement full speed astern—is what Christians call repentance. . . .

Remember, this repentance, this willing submission to humiliation and a kind of death, is not something God demands of you before He will take you back and which He could let you off if He chose: it is simply a description of what going back to Him is like. If you ask God to take you back without it, you are really asking Him to let you go back without going back. It cannot happen.

—from *Mere Christianity*

Dragged, Kicking and Screaming

In the Trinity Term of 1929, I gave in, and admitted that God was God, and knelt and prayed: perhaps, that night, the most dejected and reluctant convert in all England. I did not then see what is now the most shining and obvious thing; the Divine humility which will accept a convert even on such terms. The Prodigal Son at least walked home on his own feet. But who can duly adore that Love which will open the high gates to a prodigal who is brought in kicking, struggling, resentful, and darting his eyes in every direction for a chance of escape? The words *compelle intrare*, compel them to come in, have been so abused by wicked men that we shudder at them; but, properly understood, they plumb the depth of the Divine mercy. The hardness of God is kinder than the softness of men, and His compulsion is our liberation.

—from *Surprised by Joy*

Am I Ignoring God?

Honest rejection of Christ, however mistaken, will be forgiven and healed—'Whosoever shall speak a word against the Son of man, it shall be forgiven him' [Luke 12:10]. But to *evade* the Son of Man, to look the other way, to pretend you haven't noticed, to become suddenly absorbed in something on the other side of the street, to leave the receiver off the telephone because it might be He who was ringing up, to leave unopened certain letters in a strange handwriting because they might be from Him—this is a different matter. You may not be certain yet whether you ought to be a Christian; but you do know you ought to be a Man, not an ostrich, hiding its head in the sand.

—from 'Man or Rabbit' in *God in the Dock*

Join the Dance

Dance and game *are* frivolous, unimportant down here; for 'down here' is not their natural place. Here, they are a moment's rest from the life we were placed here to live. But in this world everything is upside down. That which, if it could be prolonged here, would be a truancy, is likest that which in a better country is the End of ends. Joy is the serious business of Heaven.

—from *Letters to Malcolm: Chiefly on Prayer*

Are My Feelings Bad?

No natural feelings are high or low, holy or unholy, in themselves. They are all holy when God's hand is on the rein. They all go bad when they set up on their own and make themselves into false gods.

—from *The Great Divorce*

_____

_____

_____

_____

_____

_____

_____

_____

_____

_____

_____

_____

_____

And What of My Feelings?

Don't bother much about your feelings. When they are humble, loving, brave, give thanks for them; when they are conceited, selfish, cowardly, ask to have them altered. In neither case are they *you*, but only a thing that happens to you. What matters is your intentions and your behaviour.

—from a letter to Genia Goelz, 13 June 1951

I Suddenly Discovered . . .

L ast week, while at prayer, I suddenly discovered—or felt as if I did—that I had really forgiven someone I have been trying to forgive for over thirty years. Trying, and praying that I might. When the thing actually happened—sudden as the longed-for cessation of one's neighbour's radio—my feeling was 'But it's so easy. Why didn't you do it ages ago?' So many things are done easily the moment you can do them at all. But till then, sheerly impossible, like learning to swim. There are months during which no efforts will keep you up; then comes the day and hour and minute after which, and ever after, it becomes almost impossible to sink.

—from *Letters to Malcolm: Chiefly on Prayer*

How Can I Forgive?

It is perhaps not so hard to forgive a single great injury. But to forgive the incessant provocations of daily life—to keep on forgiving the bossy mother-in-law, the bullying husband, the nagging wife, the selfish daughter, the deceitful son—how can we do it? Only, I think, by remembering where we stand, by meaning our words when we say in our prayers each night 'forgive us our trespasses as we forgive those that trespass against us'. We are offered forgiveness on no other terms. To refuse it is to refuse God's mercy for ourselves. There is no hint of exceptions and God means what He says.

—from 'On Forgiveness' in *The Weight of Glory*

Improve Yourself

Abstain from all thinking about other people's faults, unless your duties as a teacher or parent make it necessary to think about them. Whenever the thoughts come unnecessarily into one's mind, why not simply shove them away? And think of one's own faults instead? For there, with God's help, one *can* do something. Of all the awkward people in your house or job there is only one whom you can improve very much. That is the practical end at which to begin. And really, we'd better. The job has to be tackled some day: and every day we put it off will make it harder to begin. . . . Be sure there is something inside you which, unless it is altered, will put it out of God's power to prevent your being eternally miserable.

—from 'The Trouble with "X"' in *God in the Dock*

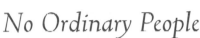

No Ordinary People

Remember that the dullest and most uninteresting person you can talk to may one day be a creature which, if you say it now, you would be strongly tempted to worship, or else a horror and a corruption such as you now meet, if at all, only in a nightmare. All day long we are, in some degree, helping each other to one or other of these destinations. It is in the light of these overwhelming possibilities, it is with the awe and the circumspection proper to them, that we should conduct all our dealings with one another, all friendships, all loves, all play, all politics. There are no *ordinary* people. You have never talked to a mere mortal. Nations, cultures, arts, civilisations—these are mortal, and their life is to ours as the life of a gnat. But it is immortals whom we joke with, work with, marry, snub, and exploit—immortal horrors or everlasting splendours.

—from 'The Weight of Glory'

To the Glory of God

I reject at once an idea which lingers in the mind of some modern people that cultural activities are in their own right spiritual and meritorious—as though scholars and poets were intrinsically more pleasing to God than scavengers and bootblacks. . . . Let us clear it forever from our minds. The work of a Beethoven and the work of a charwoman become spiritual on precisely the same condition, that of being offered to God, of being done humbly 'as to the Lord'. This does not, of course, mean that it is for anyone a mere toss-up whether he should sweep rooms or compose symphonies. A mole must dig to the glory of God and a cock must crow. We are members of one body, but differentiated members, each with his own vocation.

—from 'Learning in War-Time' in *The Weight of Glory*

Do I Live in the Present?

Screwtape explains the importance of the Present: The humans live in time but our Enemy destines them to eternity. He therefore, I believe, wants them to attend chiefly to two things, to eternity itself, and to that point of time which they call the Present. For the Present is the point at which time touches eternity. . . . He would therefore have them continually concerned either with eternity (which means being concerned with Him) or with the Present—either meditating on their eternal union with, or separation from, Himself, or else obeying the present voice of conscience, bearing the present cross, receiving the present grace, giving thanks for the present pleasure.

—from *The Screwtape Letters*

To Long for the Past

How could we endure to live and let time pass if we were always crying for one day or one year to come back—if we did not know that every day in a life fills the whole life with expectation and memory and that these *are* that day?

—from *Out of the Silent Planet*

_____

_____

_____

_____

_____

_____

_____

_____

_____

_____

_____

_____

_____

_____

Would I Still Obey?

Screwtape warns: Do not be deceived, Wormwood. Our cause is never more in danger than when a human, no longer desiring, but still intending, to do our Enemy's will, looks round upon a universe from which every trace of Him seems to have vanished, and asks why he has been forsaken, and still obeys.

—from *The Screwtape Letters*

What He Intends

The question is not what we intended ourselves to be, but what He intended us to be when He made us. He is the inventor, we are only the machine. He is the painter, we are only the picture. . . . We may be content to remain what we call 'ordinary people': but He is determined to carry out a quite different plan. To shrink back from that plan is not humility: it is laziness and cowardice. To submit to it is not conceit or megalomania; it is obedience.

—from *Mere Christianity*

_____

_____

_____

_____

_____

_____

_____

_____

_____

_____

_____

Extreme Makeover?

Imagine yourself as a living house. God comes in to rebuild that house. At first, perhaps, you can understand what He is doing. He is getting the drains right and stopping the leaks in the roof and so on: you knew that those jobs needed doing and so you are not surprised. But presently he starts knocking the house about in a way that hurts abominably and does not seem to make sense. What on earth is He up to? The explanation is that He is building quite a different house from the one you thought of—throwing out a new wing here, putting on an extra floor there, running up towers, making courtyards. You thought you were going to be made into a decent little cottage: but He is building a palace. He intends to come and live in it Himself.

—from *Mere Christianity*

Too Easily Pleased

The New Testament has lots to say about self-denial, but not about self-denial as an end in itself. We are told to deny ourselves and to take up our crosses in order that we may follow Christ; and nearly every description of what we shall ultimately find if we do so contains an appeal to desire. If there lurks in most modern minds the notion that to desire our own good and earnestly to hope for the enjoyment of it is a bad thing, I submit that this notion . . . is no part of the Christian faith. Indeed, if we consider the unblushing promises of reward and the staggering nature of the rewards promised in the Gospels, it would seem that Our Lord finds our desires not too strong, but too weak. We are half-hearted creatures, fooling about with drink and sex and ambition when infinite joy is offered us, like an ignorant child who wants to go on making mud pies in a slum because he cannot imagine what is meant by the offer of a holiday at the sea. We are far too easily pleased.

—from 'The Weight of Glory'

To Ride with Him

To shrink back from all that can be called Nature into negative spirituality is as if we ran away from horses instead of learning to ride. There is in our present pilgrim condition plenty of room (more room than most of us like) for abstinence and renunciation and mortifying our natural desires. But behind all asceticism the thought should be, 'Who will trust us with the true wealth if we cannot be trusted even with the wealth that perishes?' Who will trust me with a spiritual body if I cannot control even an earthly body? These small and perishable bodies we now have were given to us as ponies are given to schoolboys. We must learn to manage: not that we may some day be free of horses altogether but that some day we may ride bare-back, confident and rejoicing, those greater mounts, those winged, shining and world-shaking horses which perhaps even now expect us with impatience, pawing and snorting in the King's stables. Not that the gallop would be of any value unless it were a gallop with the King; but how else—since He has retained His own charger—should we accompany Him?

—from *Miracles*

Do I Complain?

What we call *hindrances* are really the raw material of spiritual life. As if the fire should call the coal a hindrance! (One can imagine a little young fire, which had been getting on nicely with the sticks and paper, regarding it as a mere cruelty when the big lumps were put on: never dreaming what a huge steady glow, how far surpassing its present crackling infancy, the Tender of the Fire designed when he stoked it.)

—from a letter to Arthur Greeves, 24 December 1930

The More Divine Love

There are two kinds of love; we love wise and kind and beautiful people because we need them, but we love (or try to love) stupid and disagreeable people because they need us. This second kind is the more divine because that is how God loves us; not because we are loveable but because He is love, not because he needs to receive but because He delights to give.

—from a letter to Mary Van Deusen, 25 May 1951

How Can I Love My Neighbour?

The rule for all of us is perfectly simple. Do not waste time bothering whether you 'love' your neighbour; act as if you did. As soon as we do this we find one of the great secrets. When you are behaving as if you loved someone, you will presently come to love him. If you injure someone you dislike, you will find yourself disliking him more. If you do him a good turn, you will find yourself disliking him less.

—from *Mere Christianity*

Good and Evil, Full Grown

The Teacher explains Time: 'Son,' he said, 'ye cannot in your present state understand eternity: . . . But ye can get some likeness of it if ye say that both good and evil, when they are full grown, become retrospective. . . . That is what mortals misunderstand. They say of some temporal suffering, "No future bliss can make up for it," not knowing that Heaven, once attained, will work backwards and turn even that agony into a glory. And of some sinful pleasure they say "Let me have but *this* and I'll take the consequences": little dreaming how damnation will spread back and back into their past and contaminate the pleasure of the sin. Both processes begin even before death. The good man's past begins to change so that his forgiven sins and remembered sorrows take on the quality of Heaven: the bad man's past already conforms to his badness and is filled only with dreariness. And that is why, at the end of all things, when the sun rises here and the twilight turns to blackness down there, the Blessed will say "We have never lived anywhere except in Heaven," and the Lost, "We were always in Hell". And both will speak truly'.

—from *The Great Divorce*

Is My Time My Own?

Screwtape reveals an elementary deception: Men are not angered by mere misfortune but by misfortune conceived as injury. And the sense of injury depends on the feeling that a legitimate claim has been denied. The more claims on life, therefore, that your patient can be induced to make, the more often he will feel injured and, as a result, ill-tempered. Now you will have noticed that nothing throws him into a passion so easily as to find a tract of time which he reckoned on having at his own disposal unexpectedly taken from him. It is the unexpected visitor (when he looked forward to a quiet evening), or the friend's talkative wife (turning up when he looked forward to a *tête-à-tête* with the friend), that throw him out of gear. Now he is not yet so uncharitable or slothful that these small demands on his courtesy are *in themselves* too much for it. They anger him because he regards his time as his own and feels that it is being stolen. You must therefore zealously guard in his mind the curious assumption 'My time is my own'.

—from *The Screwtape Letters*

Engaging God

The prayer preceding all prayers is 'May it be the real I who speaks. May it be the real Thou that I speak to'. Infinitely various are the levels from which we pray. Emotional intensity is in itself no proof of spiritual depth. If we pray in terror we shall pray earnestly; it only proves that terror is an earnest emotion. Only God Himself can let the bucket down to the depths in us. And, on the other side, He must constantly work as the iconoclast. Every idea of Him we form, He must in mercy shatter. The most blessed result of prayer would be to rise thinking 'But I never knew before. I never dreamed . . .'

—from *Letters to Malcolm: Chiefly on Prayer*

God Shows Himself

The very question 'Does prayer work?' puts us in the wrong frame of mind from the outset. 'Work': as if it were magic, or a machine—something that functions automatically. Prayer is either a sheer illusion or a personal contact between embryonic, incomplete persons (ourselves) and the utterly concrete Person. Prayer in the sense of petition, asking for things, is a small part of it; confession and penitence are its threshold, adoration its sanctuary, the presence and vision and enjoyment of God its bread and wine. In it God shows Himself to us. That He answers prayer is a corollary—not necessarily the most important one—from that revelation. What He does is learned from what He is.

—from 'The Efficacy of Prayer' in *The World's Last Night*

Prayer Is Not a Time for Pretense

It is no use to ask God with factitious earnestness for A when our whole mind is in reality filled with the desire for B. We must lay before Him what is in us, not what ought to be in us.

—from *Letters to Malcolm: Chiefly on Prayer*

To Draw Near

We must not think Pride is something God forbids because He is offended at it, or that Humility is something He demands as due to His own dignity—as if God Himself was proud. He is not in the least worried about His dignity. The point is, He wants you to know Him: wants to give you Himself. And He and you are two things of such a kind that if you really get into any kind of touch with Him you will, in fact, be humble—delightedly humble, feeling the infinite relief of having for once got rid of all the silly nonsense about your own dignity which has made you restless and unhappy all your life. He is trying to make you humble in order to make this moment possible: trying to take off a lot of silly, ugly, fancy-dress in which we have all got ourselves up and are strutting about like the little idiots we are.

—from *Mere Christianity*

Begin with Small Prayers

And perhaps, as those who do not turn to God in petty trials will have no *habit* or such resort to help them when the great trials come, so those who have not learned to ask Him for childish things will have less readiness to ask Him for great ones. We must not be too high-minded. I fancy we may sometimes be deterred from small prayers by a sense of our own dignity rather than of God's.

—from *Letters to Malcolm: Chiefly on Prayer*

Only Experience Reveals Some Truths

The process of living seems to consist in coming to realize truths so ancient and simple that, if stated, they sound like barren platitudes. They cannot sound otherwise to those who have not had the relevant experience: that is why there is no real teaching of such truths possible and every generation starts from scratch.

—from a letter to Dom Bede Griffiths, 8 May 1939

What Panics Me?

I'm a panic-y person about money myself (which is a shameful confession and a thing dead against Our Lord's words) and poverty frightens me more than anything else except large spiders and the tops of cliffs: one is sometimes even tempted to say that if God wanted us to live like the lilies of the field He might have given us an organism more like theirs! But of course He is right. And when you meet anyone who *does* live like the lilies, one *sees* that He is.

—from a letter to an American lady, 10 August 1953

The Gift of Faith

The conflict is not between faith and reason but between faith and sight. We can face things which we *know* to be dangerous if they don't look or sound too dangerous; our real trouble is often with things we *know* to be safe but which look dreadful. Our faith in Christ wavers not so much when real arguments come against it as when it *looks* improbable—when the whole world takes on that desolate *look* which really tells us much more about the state of our passions and even our digestion than about reality. . . . If we wish to be rational, not now and then, but constantly, we must pray for the gift of Faith, for the power to go on believing not in the teeth of reason but in the teeth of lust and terror and jealousy and boredom and indifference that which reason, authority, or experience, or all three, have once delivered to us for truth.

—from 'Religion: Reality or Substitute' in *Christian Reflections*

The Sin of Sadness

My own idea, for what it is worth, is that all sadness which is not either arising from the repentance of a concrete sin and hastening towards concrete amendment or restitution, or else arising from pity and hastening to active assistance, is simply bad; and I think we all sin by needlessly disobeying the apostolic injunction to 'rejoice' as much as by anything else.

—from *The Problem of Pain*

Just a Normal Day . . .

Precisely because we cannot predict the moment, we must be ready at all moments. Our Lord repeated this practical conclusion again and again; as if the promise of the Return had been made for the sake of this conclusion alone. Watch, watch, is the burden of his advice. I shall come like a thief. You will not, I most solemnly assure you you will not, see me approaching. . . . Therefore you must be ready at all times. The point is surely simple enough. The schoolboy does not know which part of his Virgil lesson he will be made to translate: that is why he must be prepared to translate *any* passage. The sentry does not know at what time an enemy will attack, or an officer inspect, his post: that is why he must keep awake *all* the time. The Return is wholly unpredictable. There will be wars and rumours of wars and all kinds of catastrophes, as there always are. Things will be, in that sense, normal, the hour before the heavens roll up like a scroll. You cannot guess it.

—from 'The World's Last Night'

Using the Right Light

Ido not find that the pictures of physical catastrophe—that sign in the clouds, those heavens rolled up like a scroll—help one so much as the naked idea of Judgment. We cannot always be excited. We can, perhaps, train ourselves to ask more and more often how the thing which we are saying or doing (or failing to do) at each moment will look when the irresistible light streams in upon it; that light which is so different from the light of the world—and yet, even now, we know just enough of it to take it into account. Women sometimes have the problem of trying to judge by artificial light how a dress will look in daylight. That is very like the problem of all of us: to dress our souls not for the electric lights of the present world but for the daylight of the next. The good dress is the one that will face that light. For that light will last longer.

—from 'The World's Last Night'

From Moment to Moment

Never, in peace or war, commit your virtue or your happiness to the future. Happy work is best done by the man who takes his long-term plans somewhat lightly and works from moment to moment 'as to the Lord'. It is only our *daily* bread that we are encouraged to ask for. The present is the only time in which any duty can be done or any grace received.

—from 'Learning in War-Time' in *The Weight of Glory*

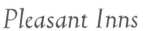

Pleasant Inns

The settled happiness and security which we all desire, God with-holds from us by the very nature of the world: but joy, pleasure, and merriment, He has scattered broadcast. We are never safe, but we have plenty of fun, and some ecstasy. It is not hard to see why. The security we crave would teach us to rest our hearts in this world and oppose an obstacle to our return to God: a few moments of happy love, a landscape, a symphony, a merry meeting with our friends, a bathe or a football match, have no such tendency. Our Father re-freshes us on the journey with some pleasant inns, but will not en-courage us to mistake them for home.

—from *The Problem of Pain*

Index of Sources Quoted